AF783684

F.Y. B.Sc. Zoology Semester Two

Practical Handbook

(Mumbai University Syllabus)

Authors

Neha Elizabeth Koshy

M.Sc., NET,

Assistant Professor, Department of Zoology, Wilson College, Chowpatty, Mumbai, Maharashtra, India

Dr. Devdatta Lad

M.Sc., M.Phil., Ph.D.,

Assistant Professor, Department of Zoology, Wilson College Chowpatty, Mumbai, Maharashtra, India

AkiNik Publications

New Delhi

Published By: *AkiNik Publications*

AkiNik Publications
169, C-11, Sector - 3,
Rohini, Delhi-110085, India
Toll Free (India) – 18001234070

Authors: *Neha Elizabeth Koshy and Dr. Devdatta Lad*

1st Edition: *2018*

Pages: *73*

ISBN: *978-93-5335-060-4*

Price: *₹545/-*

Preface

The Board of Studies in Zoology of Mumbai University introduced revised F.Y. B.Sc. syllabus into the curriculum from the academic year 2015 – 2016. Keeping the focus on the revised syllabus we like to present, F.Y. B.Sc. Zoology, Semester Two, and Practical Handbook. While preparing the handbook we authors have tried our level best to maintain a lucid language for the easy understanding of the students. We have covered up all the practical's mentioned in the revised syllabus. For the development of the handbook a number of reference books were being referred by both of us. The lists of reference books referred by us are being acknowledged in detail on the last page of the handbook. We, sincerely apologize, if any reference book is being skipped from being acknowledged. Any suggestions for enhancement are welcomed.

Authors

Neha Elizabeth Koshy and Dr. Devdatta Lad

Second Term Practical - III

Semester II Practical - IV

Second Term Practical - III

Practical - 1

Study of Survivorship Curve

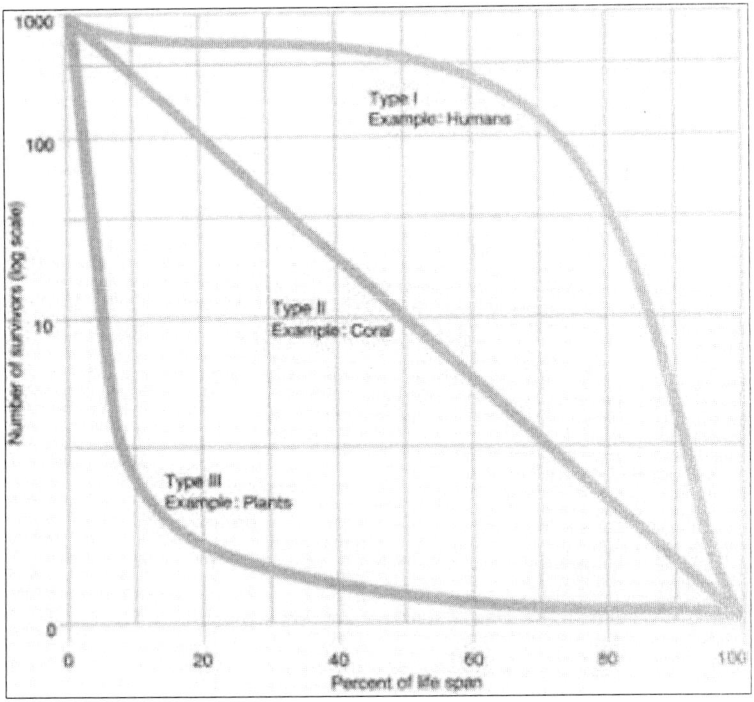

Survivorship Curves show graphically the relative survival rates of individuals at different ages. There are 3 types of survivorship curves:

- **Type I:** Individuals survive well early in life and generally live many years. At an advanced age, the death rate increases dramatically. Examples include large mammals.
- **Type II:** Individuals have a death rate that is relatively constant at any age. Examples include lizards, hydra, and some small mammals.
- **Type III:** Individuals initially have a rather low chance of survival. Those that do survive may live to an advanced age. Examples include many fish and other marine organisms.

Practical - 2

Study of Life Table

A more sophisticated method for examining population abundance is to construct a Life table. This table will have a schedule of all births and deaths in all or more likely some portion, of our population. There are two types of Life table a) Cohort (dynamic) life table, b) Static (Time specific) life table. Life table is use to know the population age structure, growth rate and its survivorship patterns. The life tables have the following variables such as:

a) X = Age/stages.

b) n_x = Number of individuals in each age/stage x.

c) l_x = Percentage of the individuals that survives to age/stage x (n_x/n_0)

d) d_x = Probability of dying during age/stage x ($l_x - l_{x+1}$)

e) q_x = Percentage of dying between age/stage x (d_x/l_x)

f) b_x = Number of offsprings produced per individual in age/stage x.

Example: Life table of spider *Apopyllus now*

X (Months)	**nx**	**Lx (n_x/n_0)**	**Dx ($l_x - l_{x+1}$)**	**Qx (d_x/l_x)**	**bx**	**lxbx**
0	250	1.000	0.500	0.500	0	0
1	125	0.500	0.156	0.312	0	0
2	86	0.344	0.072	0.209	0	0
3	68	0.272	0.060	0.221	0	0
4	53	0.212	0.188	0.887	17	3.6
5	6	0.024	0.024	1.000	34	0.8
6	0	0	0	0	0	0
			R_0			4.4

Where $R_0 = \Sigma\, l_x b_x$

R_0 has the following properties

If $R_0 > 1$, the population is increasing in size.

If $R_0 < 1$, the population is decreasing in size.

If $R_0 = 1$, the population is constant.

Exercise

Determine the population status of the given insect

X (months)	nx	Lx (n_x/n_0)	Dx ($l_x - l_{x+1}$)	Qx (d_x/l_x)	bx	lxbx
Eggs	1000				0	
Instar I	891				0	
Hibernacula	463				0	
Instar II	384				0	
Instar III -	142				0	
IV						
Pupae	7				0	
Moths	5				1050	
			R_0			

Result

Practical - 3

Calculation of Fecundity from Given Data

Fecundity is the actual reproductive rate of an organism or population measured by the number of eggs, seeds or asexual propagules. Fecundity is similar to fertility. Fecundity is important and well-studied in the field of population ecology. Fecundity can increase or decrease in a population according to current conditions and certain regulating factors.

Fecundity can be Calculated using the Given Formula

$F = N. G/g$

Where,

F = Fecundity.

G = Total weight of Ovary.

g = Total weight of subsample in sample unit.

n = Number of ova in the subsamples.

Problem

The ovary weight of Fresh water fish *Channa striatus* is 8.5 gms. When 2.5 gms of the ovary was collected and studied, it contained 1487 ova's. Calculate the fecundity of the fish.

Calculation

Practical - 4

Study of Age Structures

1) A typical means of portraying age distribution is the age pyramid.
2) An age pyramid is a vertical bar graph in which the number or proportion of individuals in various age ranges at any given time is shown from youngest at the bottom of the graph to oldest at the top.
3) An age pyramid represents the age distribution of a living population at a specific moment, thus as the population age distribution changes over a period of time, the form of the age pyramid does too.
4) From an age pyramid, one can collect the information that whether a population is expanding, contracting or stable.
5) Usually a rapidly expanding population will contain a large proportions of young individuals, a stationary population more even distribution of age classes and a declining population a large proportion of old individuals.
6) A triangular pyramid will represent a growing population and an urn shaped pyramid will indicate an increased number of middle aged and old organisms compared to the young.
7) However, a bell shaped pyramid will denote a stationary or stable population having an equal number of young and middle – age classes.

Practical - 5

Calculation of Sex Ratio from Given Data

The sex ratio is the ratio of males to females in a population. In the majority of animal species it is 1:1. But it varies from one Population to another. It always desirable to consider separately the sex ratio of important component subgroups (e.g. by race, by ethnicity). Sex Ratio is higher at very young age, the sex ratio gap narrows with increasing age and goes below 100 by middle age. The General formula for calculating the sex ratio is

$$\text{Sex Ratio} = (\text{Number of Males/Number of Females}) \times 100$$

Problems

1) In a large cattle farm there are 1063 bulls and 2784 cows. Calculate the sex ratio.
2) In a African city there are 3, 43,200 females to 3, 22, 968 males. Calculate the sex ratio of that city.

Calculations

Practical - 6

Calculation of Natality from Given Data

The Natality is equal to the number of live births in a year divided by the total population. This number is then multiplied by 1,000 to arrive at the actual Natality rate.

Therefore, the Formula for Natality Rate is

Natality rate = (number of births)/ (total population) X 1,000

Problems:

a) In 2007, there were 3,250 births in a city with population of 2,23,000. Calculate the Natality rate.

b) In 2010, there were 2,150 births in a city with population of 3,13,000. Calculate the Natality rate.

Calculations

Practical - 7

Calculation of Mortality from Given Data

The Mortality is equal to the number of deaths in a year divided by the total population. This number is then multiplied by 1,000 to arrive at the actual Mortality rate.

Therefore, the formula for Mortality rate is:

Mortality rate = (number of deaths)/ (total population) X 1,000

Problems

a) In 2011, there were 271 deaths in a city with population of 1,58,934. Calculate the Mortality rate.

b) In 2009, there were 445 deaths in a city with population of 72,072. Calculate the Mortality rate.

Calculations

Practical - 8

Calculation of Population Density from Given Data

The total number of individuals in a population residing in per unit area is called density of that population. The main factors which determine the density of any population are the natality and mortality of the population i.e. growth rate. If the growth rate is more, then the density increases and vice – versa. Density of the population is influenced by emigration and immigration. When individuals leave the population and move out it is described as emigration. As a result the density of the population decreases. When new individuals come into the population from outside, it is described as immigration. It results in increasing the density of the population. Population Density can be easily calculated by using formula as follows:

Population Density = N/A

Where, N stands for the Number of Organisms and a Stands for the area

Using the above mentioned formula calculate the Population Density for the data given in the table below.

Habitat	Area (Km^2)	No. of Individuals	No. of Individuals/Unit area(Population Density)
1	4	31	
2	6	15	

Result

Practical - 9

Estimation of Population Density by Capture Recapture Method

Aim: To estimate the population density by capture recapture method.

Requirement: Any live insect population, white ink for marking.

Principle: Population density refers to the size of population in relation to any unit of space at a particular time. There are different methods for determining the population density for a variety of organisms, capture and recapture method is one amongst them. It is mostly used for analyzing the population density of mobile organisms. It is the simplest method which is also known as Pitterson – Linken index. It is not simply an index of relative population size but a true estimate of the actual population of the area sampled.

Procedure

1) Capture, count and mark with white ink the insects from the insect population provided.
2) Take the number of insects captured, counted and marked as a.
3) Release the insects and allow them to disperse into their population.
4) Wait for around 10 minutes for complete dispersal of the insects to happen.
5) After that again recapture some insects from the same population.
6) Now count the total insects recaptured and take that value as b.
7) Also count the number of insects already marked in the recapture and consider that value as c.
8) Now calculate the population density using the formula.

$$\text{Population Density} = \frac{a \times b}{c}$$

Observation Table

S. No.	Counted	Number
1	Total captured and marked (a)	
2	Total recaptured (b)	
3	Already marked in recapture (c)	

Calculation

Result: The population density of the given insect population as per the capture-recapture method is ________.

Practical - 10

Study of J Shaped Curve

Populations have characteristic patterns of growth with time. These patterns are known as population growth forms or growth curves. There are two basic patterns namely J – shaped and Sigmoid – shaped.

In case of J – shaped growth form, there is a sudden rise in population called population explosion or exponential growth of population.

After attaining the peak value, the population may abruptly crash. This is due to the fact that the exponential growth cannot be sustained infinitely. The reason behind this is environmental resistance, so also the environment is ever changing. E.g. many insects have a large population in rainy season, which dwindles drastically at the end of the season.

Practical - 11

Study of Sigmoid Growth Curve

The Sigmoid shaped growth curve shows a gradual increase in population size initially. It is then followed by an exponential increase and then a gradual decline to a near constant level.

The slowdown, following the exponential phase occurs due to increasing environmental resistance.

The constant level is due to the zero population growth. It is designated as "K" i.e. carrying capacity. It is defined as the maximum number of individuals which the environment can support or sustain.

Practical - 12

Estimation of Hardness from Given Water Samples

Aim: To determine the hardness of different water samples by EDTA titrimetric method.

Reagents: Buffer solution, Eriochrome black T indicator, 0.01M EDTA.

Principle: EDTA forms chelated soluble complex when added to a solution of certain metal cations. If small amount of dye such as Eriochrome black T indicator is added to an aqueous solution containing calcium and magnesium ions at pH 10 the solution turns wine red. If EDTA is added as a titrant, the calcium and magnesium will be complexed. When all of the magnesium and calcium has been complexed the solution turns wine red to blue marking the end point of titration.

Procedure

1) Take 10 ml of tap water in a conical flask.
2) Add 1ml of buffer solution and shake well.
3) Add 1 to 2 drops of Eriochrome black T indicator, shake well to get wine red colour.
4) Titrate it against 0.01M EDTA by adding drop wise from the burette until the colour changes wine red to blue.
5) Repeat the procedure again with well water.

Observation Table: Tap water

Reading	Initial	Final	Difference (B.R.)
1			

Well Water

Reading	Initial	Final	Difference (B.R.)
1			

Calculation

1 meq of EDTA = 40.08 mg of Ca^{2+}

$$\text{Hardness as mg of } Ca^{2+}/L = \frac{\text{B.R. X Normality of EDTA x 40.08 x 1000}}{\text{10 (Volume of sample taken)}}$$

Result

1) Hardness of Tap water ______________________ mg of Ca^{2+}/L.
2) Hardness of Well water ______________________ mg of Ca^{2+}/L.

Practical - 13

Estimation of Free Carbon Dioxide from Given Water Samples

Aim: To estimate the amount of free carbon dioxide from given water samples.

Apparatus and Reagent: Burette, pipette, conical flask, beaker, measuring cylinder, 1/44N NaOH, 1% Phenolpthalein indicator, tap water, diluted aerated drink.

Principle: Free carbon dioxide in water forms weak carbonic acid it reacts with NaOH to form $NaHCO_3$ at pH 8.3. Hydrogen is completely displaced and pink colour appears with excess drop of NaOH in presence of Phenolpthalein.

Procedure

1) Take 100 ml of sample water in conical flask.
2) Add 2 drops of Phenolpthalein indicator.
3) Fill the burette with 1/44N NaOH solution.
4) Titrate the water sample in conical flask against 1/44N NaOH solution.
5) Endpoint is colourless to pink.
6) Repeat the procedure 3 times for tap water and diluted aerated drink.

Observation Table

Tap Water

Readings	Initial	Final	Difference	Mean
1				
2				
3				

Diluted Aerated Drink

Readings	Initial	Final	Difference	Mean
1				

2				
3				

Solution in burette - 1/44N NaOH solution.

Solution in conical flask – water sample + 2 drops of Phenolpthalein indicator.

End point – colourless to pink.

Calculation

1 ml of NaOH = 44 mg of CO_2.

$$\text{Amount of } CO_2 = \frac{\text{N x B.R. x 44 x 1000}}{\text{Volume of water in conical flask}} = \_\_\_\_\_\text{mg/L}$$

Where, N is normality of NaOH.

44 = equivalence of NaOH in CO_2.

CO_2 of tap water =

CO_2 of diluted aerated drink =

Result

The amount of CO_2 present in the tap water = _______ mg/L.

The amount of CO_2 present in diluted aerated drink = ________ mg/L.

Practical - 14

Identification and Interpretation of Aquatic Food Chains and Food Webs

The components which are involved in the transference of food energy from producers (plants) to the higher consumers (carnivorous animals) in the process of repeated eating and being eaten up is termed as food chain. A food chain is stepwise transfer of energy in the form of food.

Food chains are not isolated from each other, but are interlinked with one another, by characteristic patterns, which are called as food web.

The food chain which occurs in aquatic ecosystem is called aquatic food chain. The main function of aquatic food chain is that 1) it depicts the structure of the living components of hydrosphere. 2) It transfers energy and materials in the aquatic ecosystems.

Aquatic Food Chain

In marine ecosystem, the producers like phytoplankton and algae occupy the first trophic level. The zooplanktons occupy the second trophic level since they feed on phytoplankton. The mackerel fish feeds on the zooplankton and therefore occupy the third trophic level. The tertiary consumers like sharks and sting rays which feed on fish occupy the fourth trophic level.

Aquatic Food Web

In the aquatic food web the phytoplanktons may be eaten by various zooplanktons such as Fish larvae, mussels, copepods, clams, barnacles, etc. These zooplanktons may be eaten by jelly fish or sole fish, herrings. Bluefish or even the largest of all the animals the whales. Study of various food chains and food webs is very significant because the ultimate food production in an area depends on the type of food chain and food webs. Recently, it has been observed that various pollutants in all the environments are transferred to various organisms through the food chains.

Practical - 15

Identification and Interpretation of Terrestrial Food Chains and Food Webs

The food chain and food web that occurs on land is called terrestrial food chain and food web.

Terrestrial Food Chain

The best example of terrestrial food chain is that of a grass or green plants eaten by goat which is eaten by the man. In this case, the grass occupies the 1st trophic level (producers). The goat occupies the second trophic level (primary consumer) and man, the third trophic level (secondary consumer).

Terrestrial Food Web

In terrestrial ecosystem grass is eaten by rabbit, mouse and grasshopper. Again, grasshopper is eaten by lizard and then the lizard is eaten by the hawk. Rabbit is also eaten by hawk. In another food chain of the food web, mouse is eaten by snake which is eaten by hawk. Thus, all these food chains are interlinked to form a food web. The food web is an excellent way of showing the trophic relationship present in an ecosystem.

Practical - 16

Construction of Food Chain or Food Web Using Given Information

Construct a Food Chain from the Given Information

Data 1

Phytoplankton.

Zooplankton.

Golden anchovy fish.

Tuna fish.

Humans.

Data 2

Grass.

Grasshopper.

Frog.

Snake.

Eagle.

Construct a food web from the given information

Data 1

Hawk.

Snake.

Mice.

Rabbit.

Frog.

Insect.

Seed eating bird.

Grasshopper.

Plants.

Practical - 17

Identification and Interpretation of Ecological Pyramids of Number

Every ecosystem has a more or less definite trophic (feeding) structure consisting of a few to many trophic levels. It is also known that there is a definite relationship between different organisms at each trophic level in respect to biomass, energy and number. Elton Charles first proposed the idea of representing these trophic structures graphically by means of pyramids. The representation of the trophic structures at various trophic levels in the food chain in the form of a plot or area is called the ecological pyramid. The pyramids can be drawn according to total number of organisms, total biomass or total energy flow at each trophic. These diagrams look somewhat similar to that of the pyramids with broad bases and narrow peaks. The pyramids can therefore be of three types; pyramid of number, pyramid of biomass and pyramid of energy. However, the pyramid of number is not very accurate and proper method of studying the trophic structure since it can change due to many other factors which are not considered while plotting the graph.

Pyramid of Number

1) The pyramid of number illustrates the population density (number of individuals with respect to area) relationship within and between the trophic levels.
2) The number of individuals at each trophic level is less than the preceding one due to differences in the rate of population growth and predation of larger ones on the smaller organisms.
3) In a lake ecosystem, the lowest trophic level is occupied by large number of diatoms.
4) The second level is occupied by zooplankton like copepods, which are less in number.
5) The third and fourth levels are mostly occupied by smaller and larger fishes, which are still fewer in number.
6) Thus, there is an increase in size of the body of organisms and a decrease in their number, as we go from the base to the top of the pyramid.

Practical - 18

Identification and Interpretation of Ecological Pyramids of Biomass

Pyramid of Biomass

1) The biomass (total amount of living material) produced at each trophic level during a particular period i.e. productivity, when plotted in the form of an area, gives the pyramid of biomass.
2) It shows that the biomass is decreased from the lower to the higher trophic levels.
3) In a forest ecosystem, the first trophic level is occupied by the plants.
4) The second trophic level is occupied by the herbivores (insects, various mammals etc.) followed by the secondary consumers (mice, snakes etc.) occupying third trophic level and the tertiary consumers (beavers etc.) the fourth trophic level.
5) Let us assume that in an area of the forest during a particular period 5000 kg of plant material is produced.
6) Then the amount of primary, secondary and tertiary consumers will be about 900 kg of insects, 100 kg of mice and 1.5 kg of beavers.
7) Another common example of pyramid of biomass of a forest ecosystem is the biomass of trees, birds and insects parasites on the birds.
8) It can be seen that the biomass of all fruit eating birds is much less than the biomass of the tree.
9) Again, the biomass of the secondary consumers namely the insects like bugs, lice etc. which depend on the bird for food is much lesser than that of the birds.
10) Similarly, in an aquatic system the phytoplankton form the base of the pyramid as the producers.
11) The second, third and fourth trophic levels are occupied by zooplankton, small fishes or molluscs and larger fishes.
12) In this case also the biomass gradually decreases from the base to the apex.

13) All these pyramids are the upright pyramids of biomass.

14) However, for a short period in some aquatic ecosystem, the amount of biomass of some higher trophic level may be less than the lower one and in that case an inverted pyramid of biomass may be obtained.

15) For example, in a lake, the phytoplankton may grow in large number during summer.

16) The zooplanktons feed on them and grow in number. But in winter, the growth of phytoplankton is less and is almost negligible in areas where the surface layer gets covered with ice.

17) At that time, the total biomass of zooplankton will be more than phytoplankton and the pyramid will be an inverted pyramid of biomass.

18) But this pyramid does not give us correct picture of the tropic levels of the ecosystem for the entire period.

19) On the contrary, if such a pyramid exists for a longer period than the ecosystem collapses.

20) It is therefore important to draw the pyramid after considering the total biomass for a long period, atleast one complete year.

Practical - 19

Identification and Interpretation of Ecological Pyramids of Energy

Pyramid of Energy

1) The rate of total energy flow or productivity at successive trophic levels during a particular period when plotted in the form of an area gives the pyramid of energy.
2) It shows a decrease in the available energy at different trophic levels.
3) The energy of sun is trapped by the primary producers, the green plants.
4) This trapped energy is converted into chemical energy which in its potential form is stored in as food in the green plants.
5) In an aquatic ecosystem, the primary producers are the phytoplanktons.
6) These minute floating plants trap the solar energy.
7) The phytoplanktons are consumed by the zooplankton or small fishes which form the primary consumers.
8) The food energy is transferred from the first trophic level i.e. the producers to the second trophic level i.e. the primary consumers.
9) But at each transfer a large amount of energy is lost as heat and in other forms.
10) Therefore, the available energy is much less in the second trophic level.
11) Now, the secondary consumers, the large fishes and fish eating birds consume the primary consumers to derive energy.
12) During the process, the energy is transferred to the secondary consumers.
13) Again a large amount of energy is lost during the transfer.
14) Thus the pyramid of energy is the upright pyramid.
15) Similarly, in a terrestrial ecosystem the amount of energy trapped by

the first trophic level, the autotrophs (plants) is much larger than the second trophic level, the herbivores.

16) The least energy is noticed in the secondary consumers, the carnivores.

17) The energy can be measured in different units.

18) Let us assume that in a particular area of a forest, the total energy trapped during a particular period in 5.8×10^2 Kcal.

19) The total amount of available energy at the next trophic level in the herbivorous animal like racoons will be only 250 Kcal. and in the carnivorous skunks at the third trophic level only 5.8 Kcal.

20) Of the three types of ecological pyramids, the energy pyramid, gives the best picture of the functional nature of communities since the number and weight of organisms do not depend on the amount of fixed energy present at any level.

21) But it depends on the rate at which the food is produced or available at any level.

22) The shape of the pyramid of energy is therefore always upright.

Practical - 20

Construction of Different Types of Pyramid from Given Data

Construct Different Types of Pyramids from the Data Given Below

1)	Zooplankton	-	1000.
	Fish	-	100.
	Great white shark	-	1.
	Seal	-	10.
	Phytoplankton	-	10,000.

2)	Hawk	-	4200 Kg/Km^2.
	Grass	-	2.09×10^7 Kg/Km^2.
	Mouse	-	2100 Kg/Km^2.
	Grasshopper	-	20,925 Kg/Km^2.

3)	Phytoplanktons	-	100% energy.
	Shark	-	0.01% energy.
	Zooplanktons	-	10% energy.
	Fish	-	1% energy.
	Octopus	-	0.1% energy.

Practical - 21

Study of Endangered and Critically Endangered Species of Indian Wildlife

Great Indian Bustard (*Ardeotis nigriceps*)

Characteristic Features: The Great Indian Bustard is a large ground bird with a height of about a meter. The body is brownish in colour. The crown of the head is black. Females are smaller than the males. The males are deep sandy buff coloured. Males have a well-developed gular pouch.

Distribution: This species was formerly widespread in India. Today it is restricted to isolated pockets in Andhra Pradesh, Gujarat, Karnataka, Maharashtra, Madhya Pradesh and Rajasthan.

Habitat: The Great Indian Bustard are often found in arid and semi – arid grasslands, open country with thorn scrubs and tall grass. It avoids irrigated areas.

Status: Critically endangered.

Reasons for Decline: The main reason for the decline is hunting and habitat loss. In the past they were heavily hunted for their meat and for sport.

Asiatic lion (*Panthera leo persica*)

Characteristic Features: The most striking morphological character, which is always seen in Asiatic lions and rarely in African lions is a longitudinal fold of skin running along its belly. Asiatic lions are slightly smaller than African lions. Asiatic lions weigh about 160 Kgs. Their height is about 3.5 feets. Males have moderate mane. The fur colour ranges from sandy brown to grey.

Distribution: In the early 19th century the Asiatic lion were found in central Indian States of Rajasthan, Gujarat, Madhya Pradesh and Khandesh province of Maharashtra. Presently Asiatic lion can only be seen in the Gir National Park of Gujarat in India. As of May 2015, the lion population was estimated at 523 individuals.

Habitat: Asiatic lion occupies the large tracts of dry deciduous forest.

Status: Endangered.

Reasons for Decline: Heavy hunting of lions after the advent of firearms by Indian royalties and Britishers. Forest fire and epidemic are also responsible for their decline.

Blackbuck (*Antilope cervicapra*)

Characteristic Features: Blackbucks are slender with a head to body length of about 120 cm. Males are larger than females. Adult weight is 34 to 45 Kg. Tail is short and compressed. Both the sexes have white patches around the eyes, on the belly and on inside of the legs. And they are blackish brown on the back, the sides and the front of the neck. Only males have horns that are diverging, cylindrical, spiral and ringed.

Distribution: In the 19th century, blackbucks ranged in open plains from the base of the Himalayas to the area of Cape Camorin and from Punjab to Assam. Now – a – days the blackbucks occur only in several protected areas of India such as Gir forest National Park, Guindy National Park, Ranthambore National Park, etc.

Habitat: Blackbucks generally live on open plains and open woodlands. They are grazers and avoid forested areas.

Status: Near Threatened.

Reasons for Decline: Blackbucks were hunted for their flesh and skin. This has reduced their population considerably.

Olive Ridley Sea Turtle *(Lepidochelys olivacea)*

Characteristic Features: The olive Ridley is a small sea turtle with an adult carapace length averaging 60 to 70 cm. The carapace is heart shaped. It has paddle – like forelimbs each having two anterior claws. The upperparts are grayish green to olive in colour. Hatchlings are dark gray in colour. Olive Ridleys weigh over 50 kg. Olive Ridleys adults exhibit sexual dimorphism. Males have longer and thicker tails. Males have longer more tapered carapaces than females, which have round, dome like carapace.

Distribution: Olive Ridley turtle are found living in tropical and warm waters of the Pacific and Indian Ocean from India, Arabia, Japan, Africa, Australia and New Zealand.

Habitat: Olive Ridley turtles are found in shallow marine waters upto a depth of about 55 m. Only occasionally they can be seen in open waters.

Status: Vulnerable.

Reasons for Decline: Olive Ridley Turtles eggs are food of raccoons, dogs, pigs, ghost crabs and they prey on it. Humans are one of the major reason for their decline as they slaughter nesting females on beach for their meat and hides. Other major threats include mortality due to collision with boats, accidental fishing because of Gill net, Trawl net and Longline fishing.

Slender-Billed Vulture *(Gyps tenuirostris)*

Characteristic Features: Slender billed vulture is about 80 to 95 cm in length. This vulture is mostly grayish in colour. The thighs have whitish colour. The neck is long, bare, skinny and black coloured. The black head is angular and narrow with the presence of a dark bill.

Distribution: In India the slender billed vulture is found from Gangetic plains to Himachal Pradesh and from Orissa to Assam. It is also found in Bangladesh, Nepal, Burma and Cambodia.

Habitat: Slender billed vulture prefers flat plains and areas with availability of fresh water resources.

Status: Critically endangered.

Reasons for Decline: This species has declined drastically. The reason for decline of this species is a non – steroidal anti – inflammatory drug, Diclofenac, which is given to working farm animals. Diclofenac is highly poisonous to vultures, it causes kidney failures in them as it enters their body when they scavenge the dead bodies of the farm animals that are thrown away. Today Diclofenac is banned for farm animals in India and it is replaced by Meloxicam, which is not toxic to vultures.

Gharial *(Gavialis gangeticus)*

Characteristic Features: The gharial is characterized by presence of extremely long, thin jaws, which are considered as an adaptation to a predominantly fish diet. The gharial can reach upto 6 meters and can have a weight of about 160 kgs. They have light olive colour above with dark cross – bands and specks on the head, body and tail. Male gavials develop a hollow bulbous nasal protuberance at sexual maturity.

Distribution: Gharial once lived in all the major river systems of the Indian subcontinent. Their distribution is now limited only to rivers of the National Chambal Sanctuary, Son river sanctuary and Mahanadi river.

Habitat: Gharials are thoroughly aquatic in nature. They are generally living in flowing rivers with deep waters, high sand banks and good fish stocks. Exposed sand banks are used for nesting.

Status: Critically endangered.

Reasons for Decline: The present Gharial population is less than 235 individuals. The population has declined due to loss of riverine habitat, depletion of fish resources and entanglement in fishing nets.

Malabar Civet *(Viverra civettina)*

Characteristic Features: The Malabar large spotted civet also known as the Malabar civet is endemic to the Western Ghats of India. The Malabar large spotted civet is dusky gray in colour. It has a dark mark on the cheek, large transverse dark marks on the back and side and 2 dark lines on neck. Its throat and neck are white. Mane is present between the shoulders. Tail is ringed with dark bands. Identification of male to female is difficult. Normal weight is around 6.6 Kgs.

Distribution: In the 19th Century Malabar civets occurred throughout the Malabar Coast. Now they are rarely sighted in Kerala only.

Habitat: Malabar civet likes to inhabit the forest and richly wooded lowland and also the elevated forest tracts.

Status: Critically endangered.

Reasons for Decline: Large forest areas were cleared for cashew and rubber plantations this has lead to habitat destruction reducing their population. Also the civet were hunted and sometime reared by the Ayurvedic physicians in Kerala to obtain Civetone an extract from the scent gland which was used in medicine.

Practical - 22

Biodiversity Hotspots - Western Ghats

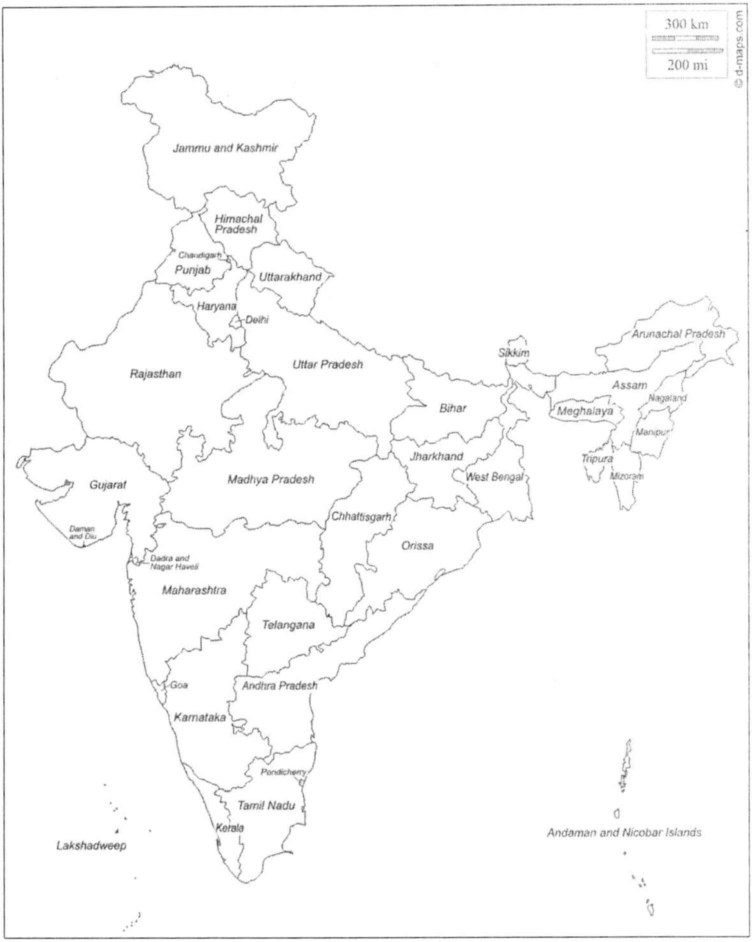

Exercise

1) In the given Map of India mark the Biodiversity hotspots - Western Ghats.

2) The Biodiversity hotspots - Western Ghats lies in which states of India.

3) Mention the various species of fauna observed in the Biodiversity hotspots - Western Ghats.

Practical - 23

Biodiversity Hotspots - Indo Burma Border

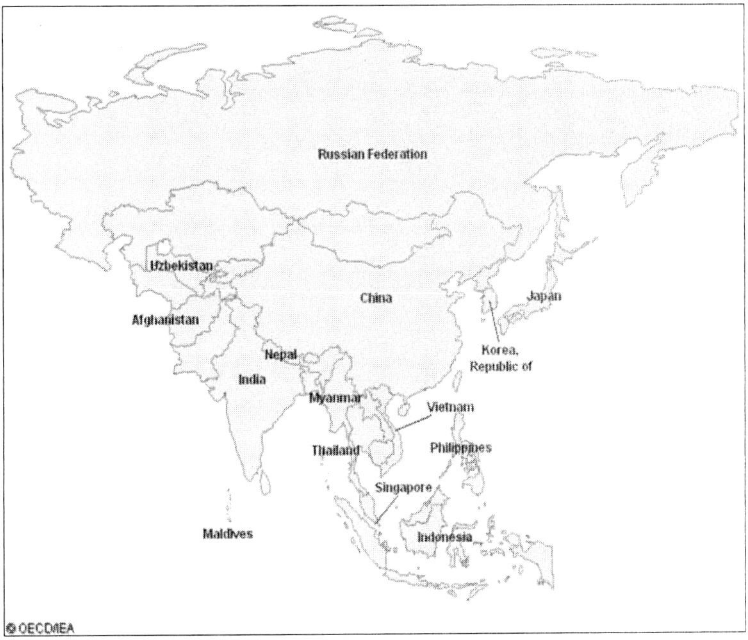

Exercise

1) In the given Map of Asia mark the Biodiversity hotspots – Indo Burma Border.
2) The Biodiversity hotspots – Indo Burma Border lies in which countries.

___

___

___

3) Mention the various species of fauna observed in the Biodiversity hotspots – Indo Burma Border.

Practical - 24

Study of Sanctuaries, National Parks and Biosphere Reserve in India

Exercise

1) In the given Map of India mark the various Sanctuaries, National Parks and Biosphere reserves situated in India.

2) In the table given below mention the various Sanctuaries, National Parks and Biosphere reserves situated in India, also mention the brand fauna observed there and the reasons for their decline.

Name of Sanctuaries, National Parks and Biosphere Reserves	Brand Fauna	Reasons of their Decline

References for Practical One

S. No.	Author	Name of the Book	Publication
1	Kotpal	Vertebrates	Rastogi Publication
2	Kotpal	Protozoa	Rastogi Publication
3	E. L. Jordan & P. S. Verma	Chordata Zoology	S. Chand Publication
4	C. L. Garg	Zoology	Manoj Publication
5	Miller and Harley	Zoology	McGraw Hill
6	S. S. Bhattacharya	Practical in Zoology	Sheth Publication
7	S. S. Bhattacharya	Textbook of Zoology	Sheth Publication
8	Ecology	Sambamurty	Narosa Publication

Semester II
Practical - IV

Practical - 1

Qualitative Estimation of Vitamin C by Iodometric Method

Aim: To estimate the vitamin C content in the given sample using iodometric method.

Requirements: Iodine Solution [potassium iodide (KI) + potassium iodate (KIO_3) + 3 M sulfuric acid (H_2SO_4)], 1% Starch Indicator Solution, Standard Vitamin C Solution 0.25% (0.250g/100ml), Unknown sample (Fresh or packaged fruit juices, fruits, vegetables, vitamin C tablets etc. can be used), burettes, pipettes, flasks.

Principle: Vitamin C (ascorbic acid) is an antioxidant that is essential for human nutrition. Vitamin C deficiency can lead to a disease called scurvy, which is characterized by abnormalities in the bones and teeth. Many fruits and vegetables contain vitamin C, but cooking destroys the vitamin, so raw citrus fruits and their juices are the main source of ascorbic acid for most people. One way to determine the amount of vitamin C in food is to use a redox titration.

A suitable method for the determination of vitamin C (ascorbic acid, $C_6H_8O_6$) is a titration with potassium iodate (KIO_3). In this reaction, potassium iodate is used as a titrant and when added to an ascorbic acid solution that contains strong acid and potassium iodide (KI), the potassium iodate reacts with potassium iodide, liberating molecular iodine (I_2) as shown in the reaction: $KIO_3 + 5KI + 6H^+ \rightarrow 3I_2 + 6K+ + 3H_2O$

During the titration, as long as the solution contains ascorbic acid, the I_2 produced in above equationis reacts with ascorbic acid to form dehydroascorbic acid ($C_6H_6O_6$) and iodide ion (I^-)

$$C_6H_8O_6 + I_2 \rightarrow C_6H_6O_6 + 2I^- + 2H^+$$

Once all the ascorbic acid has been consumed, any excess iodine (I_2) will remain in solution. This excess iodine reacts with starch, to form an intensely blue-black coloured complex, indicating that the endpoint is reached.

This titration procedure is appropriate for testing the amount of vitamin C in vitamin C tablets, juices, and fruits and vegetables. The titration can be performed using just iodine solution and not iodate, but the iodate solution is more stable and gives a more accurate result.

Procedure

1. Fill the burette with the iodine solution. Record the initial volume.
2. Take a flask and label it as standard. In this flask, add 25ml of vitamin C. Add few drops of 1% starch solution. Titrate the solution until the endpoint is reached. The proper endpoint is when the blue color persists even after 20 seconds of swirling the solution. Record the final volume of iodine solution. The volume that was required is the final volume minus the initial volume. Note down the readings. Repeat the process twice more and take the average of all 3 burette readings.
3. Take a flask and label it as unknown. In this flask, add 25ml of unknown sample. Add few drops of 1% starch solution. Titrate the solution until the endpoint is reached. The proper endpoint is when the blue color persists even after 20 seconds of swirling the solution. Record the final volume of iodine solution. The volume that was required is the final volume minus the initial volume. Note down the readings. Repeat the process twice more and take the average of all 3 burette readings.
4. Find out the concentration of vitamin C in the unknown solution by calculation using the formula.

Observations

Readings	Standard			Unknown Sample		
	1st Reading	2nd Reading	3rd Reading	1st Reading	2nd Reading	3rd Reading
Initial burette reading						
Final burette reading						
Difference (Final B.R-Initial B.R)						
Average B.R $\frac{\text{(1st+2nd+3rd reading)}}{3}$						

Formula

$$\text{Concentration of Vitamin C in unknown sample} = \frac{\text{Average B.R of Unknown Sample}}{\text{Average B.R of Standard}} \times \text{Conc. Of Std.}$$

Calculations

Concentration of Vitamin C in unknown sample = ———— X = ———— g/25ml

Concentration of Vitamin C in unknown sample = ———— X = ———— g/100 ml

Concentration of Vitamin C in unknown sample = ———— X = ———— g/l

Result: Concentration of vitamin C in unknown sample is _______.

Note: If fruit, vegetable or tablets are used as the sample, calculate the concentration of vitamin C, in mg/100g of ascorbic acid, in the sample.

Practical - 2

Study of Microscopic Structure of Starch Granules of Different Cereals (Wheat, Maize and Jowar)

Aim: To study microscopic structure of starch granules of different cereals (wheat, maize and jowar).

Requirements: Maize, wheat, jowar, iodine solution, slides, cover slips, mortar and pestle.

Principle: Besides living cell organelles, non-living cell inclusions, as a by-product of metabolism are also found within the cell. All these non-living cell inclusions are called ergastic matters. They can either be reserve materials, secretory material or excretory material. Starch grains are classified under reserve material. They are complex, insoluble carbohydrates found in plants. They are most abundant in storage organs, cereals, fruits and seeds.

Procedure

1. **For Maize Starch Grains:** Take fresh, soaked maize and cut it vertically into two halves. Take a thin section of it longitudinally along the cut surface of the grain using a sharp blade. Stain the section with iodine and mount it in water. Place cover slip and observe the slide under low power of compound microscope. The iodine will stain the starch grains, present in the endosperm of the maize, dark blue in colour.

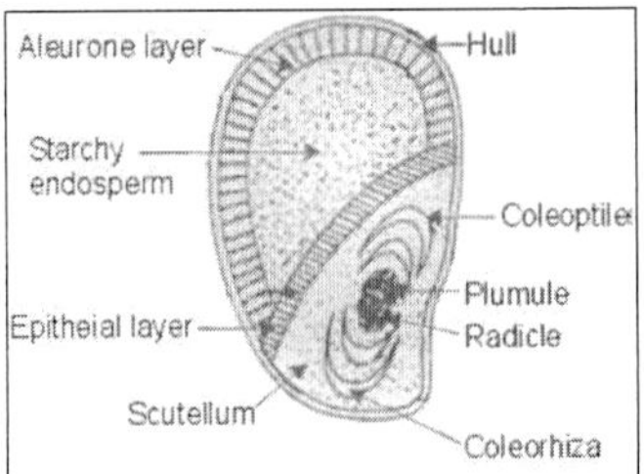

L.S. Of maize seed

2. **For Starch Grains of Other Cereals like Wheat, Rice and Jowar:** Soak the grains in water for some time. Grind a little quantity of the grains in water to prepare an extract. Take a drop of the extract onto a slide. Stain it with dilute iodine and mount it in water. Place cover slip onto the slide. Observe the slide first under low power and then under high power of compound microscope. On reaction with iodine,

only the starch granules present in the cereals will turn dark blue in colour and become visible.

3. Make a note of the structure and draw neat sketches of the starch granules present in the different cereals.

Observations

Inference

Practical - 3a)

Estimation of Maltose from Brown/White Bread

Aim: To estimate maltose in the given samples of flour used for making bread.

Requirements: Flour samples, Reagent 1-Sulphuric acid (1:5), Reagent 2- 15% sodium tungstate, Fehling's solution A ($CuSO_4$), Fehling's solution B (Na-K-tartarate in NaOH), methylene blue (1%), pipettes, flask, burette, burner.

Principle: Maltose is a disaccharide containing two glucose molecules with an α ($1 \rightarrow 4$) glycosidic linkage. Maltose can be derived from starch in food through the action of amylase. Maltose can be found in many food products, including beer, cereals, and pasta. No specific recommendations exist for maltose, and consumers should be mindful of overall sugar intake.

The current Dietary Reference Intakes recommends that 45 percent to 65 percent of your total calories should come from carbohydrates, per 1,000 calories consumed. To remain healthy, reduce added sugars as much as possible to reduce caloric intake and avoid risk for adverse health outcomes such as diabetes, cardiovascular disease and cancer, which have been linked to high sugar intake.

Procedure

1. Take 15g of flour sample A in a flask and add 15ml of water. Incubate at 27^{0}C for 1 hour. Keep shaking the flask every 15 minutes to mix the contents.
2. At the end of the digestion period, add 1.5ml of Reagent 1 H_2SO_4 and 3.5ml of Reagent 2 (sodium tungstate) to stop the reaction.
3. Filter immediately through No. 1 filter paper. Use the clear filtrate for the determination of sugar content.
4. Take 5ml of Fehling's A and 6ml of Fehling's B in a flask. Heat this mixture. Add 15ml of flour extract. Add 5 drops of methylene blue to the flask. Allow the mixture to boil for one minute.
5. Fill up the burette with the filtered flour extract.
6. Add additional flour extract from the burette slowly one drop at a

time into the flask while it is still boiling on the burner. The endpoint of the titration is when the blue colour disappears. Add an extra drop of indicator to confirm.

7. Note down the burette reading. Perform the titration again.
8. Repeat the above steps for flour sample B.
9. Calculate the maltose value by comparing the burette reading corresponding to it from the table below. Compare and comment on the maltose values found in wheat flour (white bread) and refined flour (brown bread) samples.

Observations

Readings	**Standard**		**Unknown Sample**	
	1st Reading	**2nd Reading**	**1st Reading**	**2nd Reading**
Initial burette reading				
Final burette reading				
Difference (Final B.R- Initial B.R)				
Average B.R $\frac{(1^{st}+2^{nd}\text{ reading})}{2}$				
Actual Flour extract value (Average B.R + 15 ml)				

Maltose Values Corresponding to Various Titration Levels

Flour Extract (ml)	**Maltose (mg)**	**Flour Extract (ml)**	**Maltose (mg)**
15	3.61	33	1.61
16	3.38	34	1.56
17	3.18	35	1.52
18	3.00	36	1.47
19	2.84	37	1.45
20	2.60	38	1.40
21	2.56	39	1.36
22	2.44	40	1.32
23	2.33	41	1.29
24	2.33	42	1.26
25	2.14	43	1.23
26	2.06	44	1.20
27	1.99	45	1.17
28	1.91	46	1.15

29	1.84	47	1.12
30	1.77	48	1.10
31	1.72	49	1.08
32	1.66	50	1.05

Result

The maltose content in refined flour (white bread) is ________.

The maltose content in whole wheat flour (brown bread) is ________.

Note: The maltose value of the flour should preferably be between 1.5 and 2.3.

Practical - 3b)

Moisture Content from Biscuits or Other Suitable Food Products

Aim: To determine the moisture content in the given food product.

Requirements: Biscuits or other food products like flour, bread, semolina or cereals like wheat grains or rice, oven set at 130^{0}C, desiccator, crucible or petri dish, balance.

Principle: The water content of foods varies widely. Determination of water or moisture content is one of the most important and most widely used measurements in food processing because of the significant effect of water on the stability and quality of foods. Moisture rich foods are easily susceptible to microbial attack and get spoilt quicker. Thus the shelf life of the food material is determined by the moisture content in the food. Low moisture foods usually slow down growth of microorganisms. Hence the need for analysis and control of moisture in food products.

Biscuits differ from other baked cereal products such as bread and cakes by having a low moisture content. Bread typically has 35 - 45% moisture, cake, 15 - 30%, and biscuits, 1 - 5% moisture. This low moisture content ensures that biscuits are generally free from microbiological spoilage and have a long shelf life if they are protected from absorbing moisture from damp surroundings or atmosphere.

Moisture content of food products can be determined by using various methods like direct measurement where water content is determined by removing moisture and then by measuring weight loss or/ indirect measurement in which an intermediate variable is measured and then converted into moisture content by titrations, colorimetry etc. However one of the simplest methods for determining moisture content in food products is by using direct oven drying method.

Procedure

1. Grind the biscuit or other food product into a fine powder.
2. Weigh an empty crucible or petri dish. Transfer about 5g of this

ground food product into the crucible or petri dish. Weigh again.

3. Place the food product containing petri dish or crucible into an oven set at 130^{0}C. Alternatively, a sand bath could also be used instead of the oven.
4. Remove the dishes from the oven after 1-2hrours.
5. Transfer the dishes into a dessicator and allow them to cool.
6. Weigh the dishes again after they reach room temperature.
7. Consider the loss in weight as moisture content of the food product.

Observations

1. Weight of empty crucible or petri dish = _____________
2. Weight of food product before drying (Wet weight) = _________
3. Weight of food product after drying (Dry weight) = ___________
4. Difference in weight = Wet weight – Dry weight = ___________

Formula

$$\text{Moisture content (\%)} = \frac{\text{Difference in weight}}{\text{Wet weight}} \text{ X } 100$$

Calculations

Result: Moisture content of the given food product is __________.

Practical - 4a)

Food Adulteration Test: Milk Adulterants (Starch and Glucose), Methylene Blue Reduction test (MBRT)

Aim I): To detect adulterants such as starch and glucose in milk.

Requirements: Milk samples, Lugol's iodine, 5% starch solution, Barfoed's reagent, phosphomolybdic acid reagent, test tubes, pipettes, burner.

Principle: Milk sold loose in the local market is sometimes adulterated with starch, urea, ammonium sulphateor glucose to increase the thickness of the milk and sweeten it after it is adulterated with water. Starch and urea are used to increase the specific gravity of milk so that the lactometer fails to detect the adulteration of milk with water.

Since starch reacts with iodine to form a blue coloured complex, Lugol's iodine can be used as detecting agent. If the milk turns blue, it indicates that the milk is adulterated with starch. If the milk remains white, it is unadulterated.

Glucose if present in milk reacts to give a blue colour. Glucose reduces cuprous ion to cupric ions in an acidic medium. The cuprous ions in turn reduce the colourless phosphomolybdic acid to dark blue coloured phoshomolybdous acid.

Procedure

Milk Sample	Test for Starch	Test for Glucose
Milk Sample A	5 ml of milk sample A + few drops of Lugol's iodine. Mix well and observe colour.	2 ml of milk sample A + 2 ml of Barfoed's reagent. Boil for 3-5mins. Cool the tubes. Add 1ml of phosphomolybdic acid reagent and observe the colour.
Milk Sample B	5 ml of milk sample B+ few drops of Lugol's iodine. Mix well and observe colour.	2 ml of milk sample B + 2 ml of Barfoed's reagent. Boil for 3-5mins. Cool the tubes. Add 1ml of phosphomolybdic acid reagent and observe the colour.

Observations

	Observations	Inference
Test for Starch		
Milk sample A		
Milk sample B		
Test for Glucose		
Milk sample A		
Milk sample B		

Result

Practical – 4b)

Food Adulteration Test: to Determine the Quality of Milk Sample by the Methylene Blue Reductase Test

Aim II): To detect adulterants such as starch and glucose in milk. To determine the quality of milk sample by the methylene blue reductase test.

Requirements: One raw milk sample & one pasteurized milk sample stores at room temperature for 48 hours, methylene blue solution (1:250000), test tubes, pipettes, cotton, 37^0C water bath.

Principle: A milk sample that contains a large population of actively metabolizing microorganisms will contain a markedly decreased concentration of dissolved oxygen because of the vigorous growth of the organisms. In other words, the oxidation-reduction potential of the sample is greatly lowered. The dye methylene blue, a redox indicator, loses its colour in an anaerobic environment and is said to be reduced. The methylene blue reductase test is designed to screen the quality of raw milk, which may contain large populations of enteric organisms & Streptococcus lactis, which are potent reducers of the dye. The speed at which reduction occurs following addition of methylene blue to a sample of milk indicates the milk's quality. This determination is made as follows:

Reduction Time	Quality of Milk
Less than 30 minutes	Very poor
Between 30 minutes – 2 hours	Poor
Between 2-6 hours	Fair
Between 6-8 hours	Good

Procedure

1. Label the test tubes as raw milk & pasteurized milk.
2. Using a different 10ml pipette both times, transfer 10ml of each type of milk into its appropriately labeled test tube.
3. Add 1ml of the methylene blue solution to each test tube.
4. Mix the dye well & place in the water bath.
5. Observe the milk samples for methylene blue reduction every 30

minutes for 3 to 6 hours.

6. Reduction is demonstrated by a change in the colour of the sample to white.
7. Record the time required for reduction in both milk samples.
8. Based on your observations, determine & record in the chart the quality of each sample.

Observations

	Raw Milk	**Pasteurized Milk**
Reduction Time		
Quality of Milk		

Inference

Practical - 4c)

Food Adulteration Test: Adulterants in Cheese, Butter, Jaggery, Ghee, Honey, Iodized Salt

Aim: To detect adulterants in food stuffs like cheese, butter, jaggery, ghee, honey and iodized salt.

Requirements: Butter, jaggery, honey, ghee, cheese, iodized salt, iodine, dil. H_2SO_4, conc. HCl, ether, resorcinol, aniline chloride, muratic acid, iodine solution, Lugol's iodine solution, test tubes, pipettes, burner, petri dish etc.

Principle: Food adulteration is an act of intentionally debasing the quality of food offered for sale either by the admixture or substitution of inferior substances or by the removal of some valuable ingredient. Food adulteration takes into account not only the intentional addition, substitution or removal of substances which adversely affect nature, substances and quality of foods, but also their incidental contamination during the period of growth, harvesting, storage, processing, transport and distribution.

"Adulterant" means any material which is or could be employed for making the food unsafe or sub-standard or mis-branded or containing extraneous matter. Food is adulterated if its quality is lowered or affected by the addition of substances which are injurious to health or by the removal of substances which are nutritious. Food is declared adulterated if: (i) A substance is added which injuriously affects it (ii) Cheaper or inferior substances are substituted (iii) It is an imitation (iv) It is coloured or otherwise treated, to improve its appearance or if it contains any added substance injurious to health (v) Its quality is below the standard

Adulterated food is dangerous because it may be toxic and can affect health and it could deprive nutrients essential for proper growth and development. Very often food is adulterated by merchants and traders who want to make a quick profit. But shortages and increasing prices, consumer demands for variety in foods, a lack of awareness, negligence, among consumers and inadequate enforcement of food laws and food safety measures also lead to food adulteration.

Some of the common adulterated foods are milk and milk products, Atta, edible oils, cereals, condiments (whole and ground), pulses, coffee, tea, confectionary, baking powder, non-alcoholic beverages, vinegar, besan and curry powder.

Procedure

Food Product	Adulterant	Method of detection	Remarks
Ghee cottage cheese	Coal Tar Dyes	Add 5 ml of dil. H_2SO_4 or conc. HCl to one teaspoon full of melted sample in a test tube. Shake well.	Pink colour (in case of H_2SO_4) or crimson colour (in case of HCl) indicates coal tar dyes. If HCl does not give colour dilute it with water to get the colour
Ghee, Butter	Vanaspati or Margarine	Take about one tea spoon full of melted sample with equal quantity of concentrated HCl in a test tube and add a pinch of sugar. Shake for one minute and let it stand for five minutes.	Appearance of crimson or red colour in lower acid layer after adding and shaking with sugar, then Vanaspati or Margarine is present
Ghee, Butter	Mashed potatoes, sweet potatoes or other starches	Add a few drops of Iodine, which is brownish in colour	The iodine turns blue in colour if potatoes or other starches are present.
Honey	Water, molasses	Dip a cotton wick in honey and light it with a match.	If it burns, then the honey is pure. If adulterated, the presence of water will not allow the honey to burn and will produce a crackling sound.
Honey	Invert sugar, jaggery	Fiehe test: Add 5 ml of ether to equal amount of honey and shake the mixture well. Decant the ether and let the remaining mixture evaporate in a petri dish at room temperature. To this add 3 ml of resorcinol	If the honey contains invert sugar then the acid layer would turn pink at first and cherry red in about 20 minutes.
Honey	Sugar	Aniline Chloride Test: Take 5 ml. Of honey in a porcelain dish. Add Aniline chloride solution and stir.	Orange red colour indicates presence of sugar
Honey	Glucose	Iodine test: Dilute the honey with equal amount of water. Add few drops of iodine solution and observe	Presence of additional glucose would turn the mixture red or violet but the pure honey would

		the colour.	remain unchanged
Iodized salt	Common salt	Cut a piece of potato, add salt and wait a minute. Add two drops of lemon juice and observe colour.	If salt is iodized, blue colour will develop. In case of common salt, there will be no blue colour.

Food Product	Adulterant	Method of Detection	Remarks
Jaggery	Sodium bicarbonate	Take ¼ tea spoon of the jiggery in a test tube. Add 3 ml of Muratic acid and observe.	The presence of sodium bicarbonate causes effervescence.
Jaggery	Metanil yellow colour	Take ¼ of a teaspoon of the Jiggery in a test tube. Add 3 ml of alcohol and shake the tube vigorously to mix up the content. Pour 10 drops of HCl in it.	A pink colouration indicates the presence of metanil yellow colours in jaggery.
Jaggery	Washing soda, chalk powder	Add a few drops of conc. solution of HCl.	Effervescence shows presence of Washing soda or chalk powder.

Make a table to note down your observations and inference for the above food adulterant tests.

Practical - 5a)

Estimation of Protein Content of Two Egg Varieties

Aim: To determine the protein content in different varieties of egg by Folin-Lowry method.

Requirements: Standard protein solution of Bovine Serum Albumin (BSA)- 0.2mg/ml, Alkaline $CuSO_4$ reagent (Reagent A- 0.5gm $CuSO_4$ in 100ml D/W; Reagent B- 1gm Na-K tartarate in 100ml D/W; Reagent C- 2gm of Na_2CO_3 in 100ml of 0.1 N NaOH) Mix 1:1 proportion of reagent A & B. Take 1ml of this mixture and add it to 50ml of reagent C to get Alkaline Cu reagent. Folin- Ciocalteau reagent -1:2 dilution in D/W, Egg white of both country and farm egg- 1:40 dilution, test tubes, pipettes, colorimeter.

Principle: Egg white is a type of protein known as albumin. When this protein solution is treated with alkaline $CuSO_4$ reagent, it forms Biuret complex with 20 or more peptide bonds. On addition of a reagent called Folin-Ciocalteau which contains phosphomolybdic acid it forms a blue colored complex. This is due to reduction of Mo^{-6} to Mo^{-4} by amino acids like tyrosine and tryptophan present in the protein. This intense blue colour is estimated colorimetrically at 620nm. Intensity of colour varies with the concentration of protein in the sample.

Procedure

If a standard graph is used, only 3 test tubes will be needed to perform the experiment. To estimate protein content in the sample by calculation method, 4 test tubes will be needed to perform the experiment. Prepare a set of 4 test tubes as follows:

Reagent	Blank	Standard	Unknown A (Farm)	Unknown B (Country)
Distilled water	1ml	-	-	-
Standard	-	1ml	-	-
protein (BSA)				
Egg white	-	-	0.5ml egg white	0.5ml egg white
solution			A	B
Alkaline $CuSO_4$	5 ml	5 ml	5 ml	5 ml
	Incubate at room temperature for 5 mins			
Folin-Ciocalteau	0.5 ml	0.5 ml	0.5 ml	0.5 ml

Mix well and incubate at room temperature for 45 mins. Read absorbance at 620 nm.

Observations

Solution	Optical Density
Blank	
Standard	
Unknown A (Farm)	
Unknown B (Country)	

Formula

$$\text{Conc. of protein in unknown} = \frac{\text{O.D of unknown X dilution factor X concentration of standard}}{\text{O.D of standard X Volume of unknown sample}}$$

$$\text{Conc. of protein in unknown} = \frac{\text{O.D of unknown X 40 X 0.2}}{\text{O.D of standard X 0.5}}$$

Calculation

Conc. of protein in unknown A (Farm egg) = ________________ = mg/ml

Conc. of protein in unknown B (Country egg) = ______________ = mg/ml

Result: On comparison of the values of protein in the two different varieties of egg are:

Farm egg = ______mg protein/ml Country egg = ______mg protein/ml

Inference

Practical - 5b)

Study of Efficacy of Different Antacids (Any Two Antacids)

Aim: To study the efficacy of different antacids.

Requirements: 0.1 M HCl, different antacids, universal BDH indicator, burettes, pipettes.

Principle: The human stomach produces approximately 1-2litres of 0.155M HCl a day. The role of this acid is to enable the digestion of proteins in the stomach and also to prevent many bacteria from surviving in the stomach. HCl catalyzes the formation of a protein digesting enzyme called pepsin. In order for pepsin to be effective, the pH of the stomach must remain below 3.0. Under situations of stress or over-eating, the pH can drop to 1.0 or less. When this occurs, the stomach becomes hyperacidic and an upset stomach or heartburn can result. Prolonged hyperacidity can result in the erosion of the stomach lining – a condition known as a peptic ulcer. Antacids are any group of drugs that neutralize acid in the digestive system. They help relieve or prevent pain by neutralizing acid. This relieves symptoms of excess acid, like acidity, indigestion or burning sensation in the chest and throat called heartburn. Antacid remedies contain substances such as: calcium carbonate, aluminium hydroxide, sodium bicarbonate, magnesium hydroxide.

In this experiment, an antacid tablet is mixed with water and a coloured chemical called an indicator. The indicator changes colour depending on whether an acid or a base is present. Then acid is slowly added to the solution to determine how much acid can be neutralized by the antacid tablet. Several different types of antacids are tested to compare the effectiveness of various products.

Procedure

1. Crush the recommended dose of the antacid tablet using a mortar and pestle into a fine powder. Transfer the powder to a flask. Put 100ml of distilled water into the same flask and shake it until the antacid is completely dissolved.
2. Add enough universal indicator to the solution in the flask to produce a noticeable colour. This should be about 10 to 15 drops. Note down the colour of the solution.

3. Fill the burette with 0.1 M HCl. Record the initial volume before starting the titration.
4. Add one drop at a time of 0.1 M HCl to the flask, swirl the contents of the flask.
5. At some point, adding drops of HCl will cause the colour of the solution in the flask to change. If the original colour returns, continue carefully adding acid only one drop of acid at a time, swirl until the colour change is permanent. The end point of the reaction is when the colour changes to neutral colour on the indicator chart.
6. Record the number of ml at the endpoint and then determine how much acid can be neutralized by the antacid tablet.
7. Repeat steps 1 to 6 with the different brands of antacid. Compare the amount of acid that can be neutralized by the different antacids and determine which is more effective in controlling acidity.

Observations

Readings	**Antacid Tablet Brand 1**	**Antacid Tablet Brand 2**
Initial burette reading		
Final burette reading		
Difference (Final B.R- Initial B.R)		

Antacid Tablet Brand and Chemical Composition	**Mass of Antacid Tablet**	**Initial Colour and pH of the Solution**	**Amount of HCl the Antacid Was Able to Neutralize (Final B.R- Initial B.R)**	**Final Colour and pH of the Solution**

Result

Practical - 6

Study of Human Parasites

Aim: To study human parasites.

Requirements: Photographs or specimens of human parasites

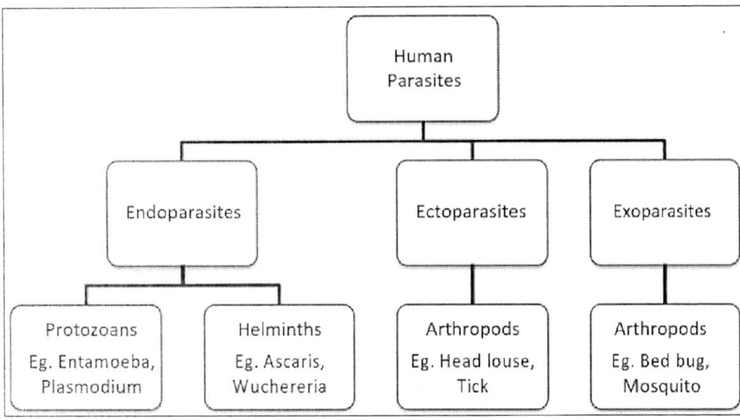

1. Entamoeba Histolytica

1. *Entamoeba histolytica* is a protozoan endoparasite.
2. It is a monogenetic parasite i.e. its entire life cycle is completed in only one host which is man. The life cycle of *Entamoeba histolytica* does not require any intermediate host.
3. It is responsible for a disease called amoebiasis. It occurs usually in the large intestine and causes internal inflammation.
4. The adult stage is called the trophozoite. The active (trophozoite) stage exists only in the host and in fresh loose faeces. Mature cysts are passed in the faeces of an infected human. Cysts survive outside the host in water, in soils, and on foods, especially under moist conditions.
5. It is seen mostly in tropical countries and in areas of poor sanitation.
6. Mode of transmission occurs when the encysted stage enter into

humans via faeco-oral route. Another human can get infected by ingesting the cysts in faecally contaminated water, food, soil or by unclean hands.

7. Infection can be asymptomatic or can lead to amoebic dysentery or amoebic liver abscess. Symptoms can include dysentery, bloody diarrhea, weight loss, fatigue, abdominal pain, and anaemia. The parasite can actually bore into the intestinal wall, causing lesions and intestinal symptoms, and then it may reach the blood stream.

   From there, it can reach different vital organs of the human body, usually the liver, but sometimes the lungs, brain, spleen, etc. A common outcome of this invasion of tissues is a liver abscess, which can be fatal if untreated.

8. Diagnosis is by stool tests or by testing for certain antigens in the blood. Treatment for amoebiasis in tissues with either metronidazole, tinidazole or chloroquine, while luminal infection is treated with iodoquinoline.

2. Plasmodium

1. Plasmodium is a protozoan endoparasite. It causes the disease malaria in man.
2. It has different species like P.vivax, P.malariae, P.ovale and P. falciparum.
3. The parasite always has two hosts in its life cycle: female Anopheles mosquito is the primary host and man is the secondary host.
4. Female Anopheles mosquito is the vector or transmission agent of malaria.
5. The life-cycle is very complex, involving a sequence of different stages both in the vector and the host.
6. Sporozoites from the saliva of a biting female mosquito are transmitted to the blood of the recipient. In humans, Plasmodium resides in liver cells and RBCs and reproduces asexually by going through many stages like merozoite, trophozoite and gametocyte. Gametocytes are taken up by the by the female mosquito when they feed on the blood of an infected human host. Within the mosquito they undergo many stages to finally form the sporozoites. These sporozoites migrate to the salivary glands of the mosquito where they are injected into the blood of the next host the mosquito bites.
7. Symptoms of malaria include high fever, chills, rigors, sweating etc.

Diagnosis is done by examination of blood smear slides which show presence of plasmodium parasite in trophozoite or signet ring stages.

8. Treatment is by administration of anti-malarial drugs like quinine, chloroquine, primaquine, proguanil, mefloquine etc.

3. Ascaris Lumbricoides

1. Ascaris is an endoparasitic helminth worm. This nematode is also known as the small intestinal roundworm.
2. One species, *Ascaris lumbricoides*, affects humans and causes the disease ascariasis.
3. A. lumbricoides is the largest intestinal roundworm and is the most common helminth infection of humans worldwide.
4. Adult worm is cylindrical shape, creamy white or pinkish in colour. Male is average 15–30 cm, has a curved end and is more slender than female. Femaleis average 20– 35 cm in length with diameter of about 5mm.
5. Infection occurs by eating food or water contaminated with Ascaris eggs. Ingestion of infective eggs from soil contaminated with human faeces or contaminated vegetables and water is the primary route of infection.
6. The eggs hatch in the intestines, burrow through the gut wall, and migrate to the lungs via the blood. There they break into the alveoli and pass up the trachea, where they are coughed up and swallowed. The larvae then pass through the stomach for a second time into the intestine where they become adult worms.
7. Most people who are infected with only a small number of worms have no symptoms. As larval stages travel through the body, they may cause tissue damage, inflammation, enlargement of the liver, spleen, or lungs. Adult worms may cause allergies or intestinal blockage.
8. Diagnosis is usually when the host passes a worm in the stool or the eggs can be seen in stool tests. Medications that are used to kill roundworms are called ascaricides. Those recommended for ascariasis are: albendazole, mebendazole, levamisole and piperazine.

4. Wuchereria Bancrofti

1. *Wuchereria bancrofti* is a helminth endoparasitic worm that is the major cause of lymphatic filariasis.

2. It is spread by a mosquito vector.
3. *W. bancrofti* carry out their life cycle in two hosts. Human beings serve as the definitive host and mosquitoes as their intermediate hosts
4. The infection spreads from person to person by mosquito bites. The adult worm lives in the human lymph vessels and produces millions of microfilariae. Microfilariae circulate in the person's blood and infect the mosquito when it bites a person who is infected. Microfilariae grow and develop in the mosquito. When the mosquito bites another person, the larval worms pass from the mosquito into the human skin, and travel to the lymph vessels. They grow into adult worms, a process that takes 6 months or more. An adult worm can live for about 5–7 years.
5. A wide range of mosquitoes can transmit the parasite, depending on the geographic area. In Asia, the most common vector is *Culex*.
6. A blood smear is a simple and fairly accurate diagnostic tool. Treatment involves the use of therapeutic drugs, such as diethylcarbamazine (DEC), ivermectin, or albendazole.
7. If the infection is left untreated, it can develop into a chronic disease called elephantiasis. This is caused by fluid collection (lymphedema) because of improper functioning of the lymph system resulting in swelling, hardening and thickening of the skin. This mostly affects the legs but can also occur in the arms.
8. Filarial infection can also cause an asthmatic disease called tropical pulmonary eosinophilia syndrome. Symptoms of tropical pulmonary eosinophilia syndrome include cough, shortness of breath, and wheezing.
9. Protection is similar to that of other mosquito-spread illnesses; one can use barriers both physical (a mosquito net), chemical (insect repellent). Prevention focuses on protecting against mosquito bites in endemic regions. Insect repellents and mosquito nets are useful to protect against mosquito bites.

5. Head Louse

1. The head louse (Pediculus humanus capitis) is an obligate ectoparasite of humans.
2. Head lice are tiny, wingless insects that spend their entire life on the human scalp and feed and feeding exclusively on human blood.
3. Humans are the only known hosts of this specific parasite. They don't

spread disease, although their bites can make a scalp itchy and irritated, and scratching can lead to infection.

4. Lice eggs are called nits. These look like tiny yellow, or brown dots before they hatch. Lice lay nits on hair shafts close to the scalp. Nits look sort of like dandruff, only they can't be removed by brushing or shaking them off.
5. The adult louse is grayish-white or tan in colour. Nymphs are smaller and become adult lice about 1 to 2 weeks after they hatch. If head lice is not treated, this process repeats itself about every 3 weeks.
6. All lice are blood-feeders and bite the skin four to five times daily to feed. They inject saliva which contains an anti-coagulant and suck blood.
7. With lice bites come itching and scratching. This is actually due to a reaction to the saliva of lice.
8. Normally head lice infest a new host only by close contact between individuals. Head-to-head contact is by far the most common route of lice transmission.
9. Head lice can be removed by combing with a fine comb or by insecticides like lindane, Malathion, carbaryl, pyrethrum, pyrethroids.

6. **Tick**

1. Ticks are arachnid ectoparasites living on the blood of mammals and other animal hosts.
2. Ticks are vectors for a number of diseases that affect both humans and other animals.
3. Tick species are widely distributed around the world, but they tend to flourish more in countries with warm, humid climates.
4. Ticks satisfy all of their nutritional requirements as ectoparasites, feeding on a diet of blood. They are obligate hematophages, needing blood to survive and move from one stage of life to another. Ticks unable to find a host to feed on will die.
5. Tick-borne illnesses are caused by infection with a variety of pathogens, including bacteria, viruses, and protozoa. Because ticks can harbour more than one disease-causing agent, patients can be infected with more than one pathogen at the same time.
6. Major tick-borne diseases include Lyme disease, Colorado tick fever, Rocky Mountain

7. Spotted Fever, African tick bite fever, tularemia, tick-borne relapsing fever, babesiosis, ehrlichiosis, and tick-borne meningo-encephalitis.
8. The best way to remove an adult tick is by freezing it off with a medical wart remover or with fine-tipped tweezers. It is important to disinfect the bite area thoroughly after removal of the tick. Oral antibiotics may be prescribed for some diseases. Other treatments may involve fluids and medications given by IV, and admission to the hospital.

7. Bed Bug

1. Bed bugs are parasitic insects that feed exclusively on blood. *Cimex lectularius*, the common bed bug, is the best known, as it prefers to feed on human blood. Other *Cimex* species feed on other animals.
2. The name "bed bug" comes from its preferred habitat of warm houses and especially near or inside beds and bedding.
3. Bed bugs are mainly active at night, but are not exclusively nocturnal. They usually feed on their hosts without being noticed. They feed by piercing the skin and withdrawing blood through an elongated beak.
4. Bed bug bites are painless at first, but later turn into itchy welts. A number of adverse health effects may result from bed bug bites, including skin rashes, psychological effects, and allergic symptoms.
5. They are not known to transmit any pathogens as disease vectors.
6. Adult bed bugs are light brown to reddish-brown, flattened, oval-shaped. Bed bugs have segmented abdomens with microscopic hairs that give them a banded appearance. Adults grow to 4–5 mm long and 1.5–3 mm wide.
7. Bed bugs are obligatory hematophagous (bloodsucking) insects. After feeding, however, their bodies swell and are a reddish color. Typically they try to feed at five- to ten-day intervals. Although under certain conditions adult bed bugs can live for five months to over a year without feeding.
8. Eradication of bed bugs requires a combination of mechanical approaches and the occasional use of pesticides. A combination of heat and drying treatments is most effective. Pesticides that have been found effective include pyrethroids, dichlorvos, and Malathion.

8. Mosquito

1. Mosquitoes are small, winged insects which comprise the family Culicidae.

2. Females of most species are ectoparasites, whose tube-like mouthparts (called a proboscis) pierce the hosts' skin to consume blood.
3. Typically, both male and female mosquitoes feed on nectar and plant juices, but in many species the mouthparts of the females are adapted for piercing the skin of animal hosts and sucking their blood as ectoparasites.
4. Female of many species feed on the blood of various kinds of hosts, mainly vertebrates, including mammals, birds, reptiles.
5. Mosquitoes go through four stages in their lifecycles: egg, larva, pupa, and adult. In most species, adult females lay their eggs in stagnant water.
6. The saliva of the mosquito often causes an irritating rash that is a nuisance.
7. Mosquitoes can act as vectors for many diseases and parasites. Infected mosquitoes carry these organisms from person to person without exhibiting symptoms themselves. Mosquito-borne diseases include viral diseases, such as yellow fever, dengue fever, and chikungunya, transmitted mostly by *Aedes* mosquito. The parasitic disease malaria, caused by various species of *Plasmodium*, is carried by female Anopheles mosquitoes. Lymphatic filariasis (elephantiasis) can be spread by a wide variety of mosquito species like *Culex*.
8. Prevention of mosquito borne diseases can be achieved by elimination of breeding places of mosquitoes. Biological control is the use of natural enemies to manage mosquito populations. Various small fishes, such as species of *Gambusia* and guppies eat mosquito larvae. Window screens and mosquito nets are the most effective measures for residential areas. Insect repellents applied on skin and give short-term protection against mosquito bites. Insecticide spraying to kill adult mosquitoes is also used.

Practical - 7

Screening of Anaemic/Non-Anaemic Persons using $CuSO_4$ Method

Aim: To screen anaemic and non-anaemic persons using $CuSO_4$ method.

Requirements: Copper Sulphate working solution with a specific gravity 1.053, Glass capillaries, Blood sample or sterile cotton, alcohol and sterile disposable lancets, Containers with 1% sodium hypochlorite solution for disposal of sharp lancets, Coplin jar with lid.

Principle: The copper sulphate method for haemoglobin determination is a qualitative screening test based on specific gravity. The density of the drop of blood is directly proportional to the amount of haemoglobin it contains. The specific gravity of the given blood sample is determined by comparing the specific gravity of a drop of blood with that of solutions of known specific gravity by Van Syke's falling drop method.

A specific gravity of 1.053 corresponds to the haemoglobin concentration of 12.5gm/dl. Hence CuSO4 solution of specific gravity 1.053 is used. The principle of the test is that when the drop of blood dropped into copper sulphate solution, it becomes encased in a sack of copper proteinate, which prevents any change in the specific gravity for about 15 seconds. Therefore, if the haemoglobin is equal to or more than 12.5 gm/dl the drop will sink within 15 seconds. If the blood drop hesitates and remains suspended in the middle or starts to rise to the top of the solution, then the haemoglobin level is below 12.5 gm/dl. This is not a quantitative test and will only show that the haemoglobin is equal to, below, or above acceptable limits. Hence it is only used as a preliminary test at the time of blood donation to screen possible donors.

Background Information: Haemoglobin is the substance in red blood cells which carries oxygen to the tissues. The normal Hb levels are 12-15gm/dl in women and 14-17g/dl in men. A low concentration of haemoglobin indicates anaemia in the person. A diet rich in iron and vitamin C, vitamin B12, and folic acid is recommended for managing anaemia. These can be taken as vitamin supplements, iron tablets or by adding certain foods to your diet. Dietary recommendations include consuming meat, green leafy vegetables, lentils, nuts, eggs, dairy products, cereals etc. If the haemoglobin is very low this is indicative of some underlying condition which should be evaluated by their physician as soon as possible.

Procedure

1. Add about 30 ml copper sulphate working solution in a clean, dry coplin jar.
2. Use the blood sample provided to you in the vial or alternatively use your own blood. If using your own blood, clean the fingertip thoroughly with alcohol and allow it to air dry. Prick the fingertip firmly with a sterile disposable lancet. Ensure a good free flow of blood. Do not squeeze the puncture site repeatedly since it may dilute the drop of blood with excess tissue fluid and gives false low results. Wipe out the first blood drop and allow the blood sample to fill up to ¾ of the microcapillary by capillary force and avoid any air bubbles.
3. Allow one blood drop to fall gently from the capillary at the height of about 1 cm above the surface of the copper sulphate solution into the coplin jar. If blood is dropped from a greater height, it will sink to the bottom because of its greater momentum.
4. Observe the blood drop for 15 seconds and note down your observations.
5. Dispose of the lancet and capillaries in a container with 1% sodium hypochlorite solution.

Observations

Blood Sample	Behaviour of Blood Drop in $CuSO_4$ Solution of Specific Gravity 1.053	Hb Level

Result: Concentration of haemoglobin in blood sample is ________ gm/dl.

Inference

Practical - 8

First Aid-Demonstration Practical Training for Teachers and Students to be Conducted by the Experts from Red Cross, Civil defence, Civic Authorities

Practical - 9

BMI Analysis-Measurement of Height/Weight and Calculation of BMI Using Formula, Preparation and Submission of Report. (10 Students/Group-50 Readings/Group)

References for Practical Two

S. No.	Author	Name of the book	Publication
1	David T. Plummer	Introduction to Practical Biochemistry	Tata McGraw Hill
2	B. K. Mahajan	Methods in Biostatistics	Jaypee Publications
3	R. C. Dubey	A Textbook of Biotechnology	S. Chand Publication
4	S.K. Sawhney & Randhir Singh	Introductory Practical Biochemistry	Narosa Publishing House
5	Dr. P. K. Bajpai	Biological instruments and methodology	S. Chand company Ltd.